WHITE

CONTENTS

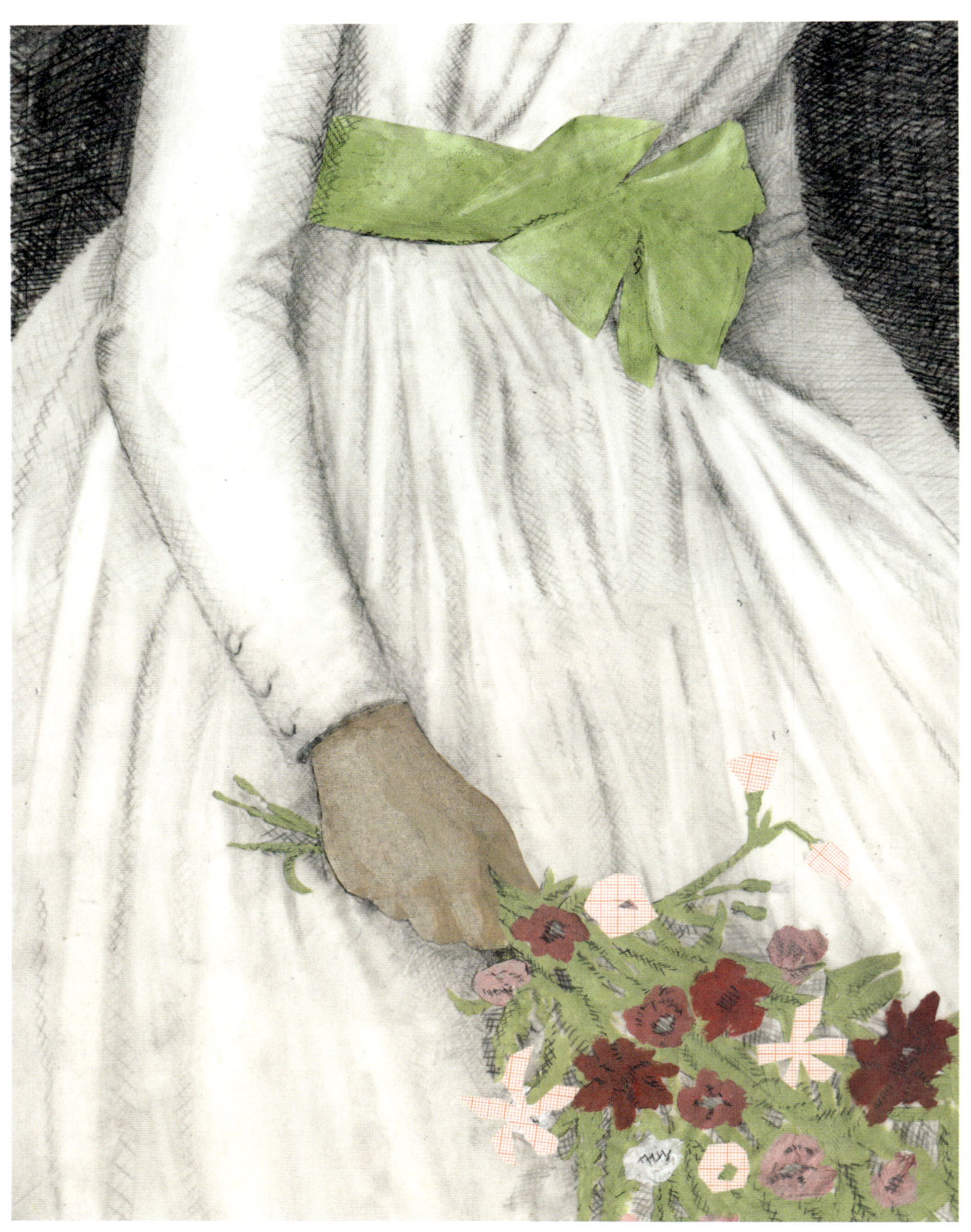

Jacques-Louis David, *Madame Pierre Seriziat (née Emilie Pecoul) with her Son* (1795), The Louvre, Paris

THE COLOR OF ALL COLORS

"You must look at all of life with the eyes of a child." (Henri Matisse, 1953)

This book introduces you to white. White is silent, tidy and calm; we could almost call it "universal". Before we begin, however, many would contest whether white is actually a color. It could be considered a non-color, since it often suggests an absence of something: white nights, when it doesn't get completely dark, or white as a sheet, when someone is very pale and lacks color. In fact, the reverse is true: white contains everything, even all the other colors. So let's try and get to know it better.

We will discover many different whites – from chalk white to snow white – see just some of the places we traditionally find it – in clouds, angels and wedding dresses – and try out ways of using white in our drawing and painting.

Throughout the book, you will find spaces to extend drawings, try out suggested exercises, make your own sketches or notes and write your impressions about what you see, notice, and think. Make sure you always have a notebook with you so you never lose a creative idea or impression.

THE COLOR WHEEL

Artists have always enjoyed arranging colors, from the lightest to the darkest, from one shade to another, in countless different ways. After many attempts, they finally settled on the color wheel as the most effective way of creating an orderly range of colors. The wheel contains all the colors in the sequence in which they merge one into another.

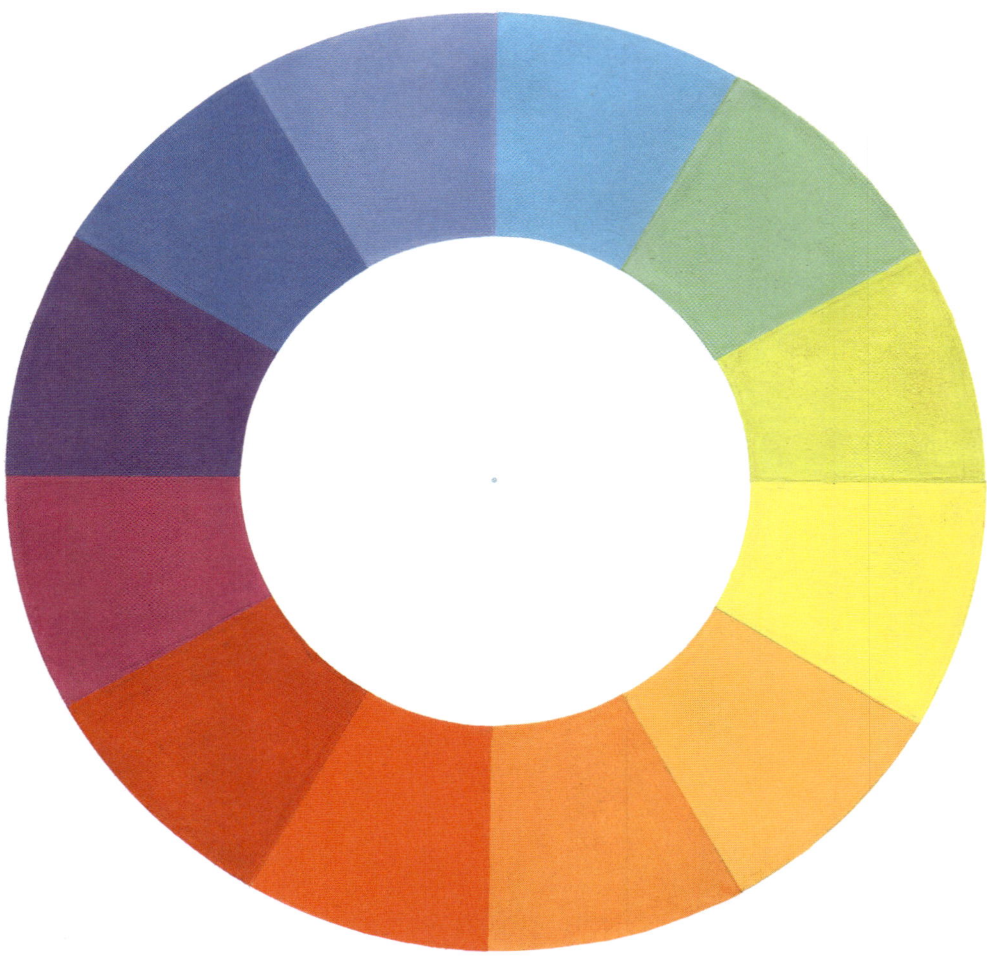

Johann Wolfgang Goethe, Color wheel from *The Theory of Colors*, 1810

Painting a Color Wheel

If you want to paint a color wheel, you must start with the three primary colors: red, yellow, and blue. Paint them at equidistant points around your circle. Then, by mixing two of them together, you'll obtain the secondary colors, which you paint in the spaces between them. Continue in the same way to create the tertiary colors, as you can see in the illustration.

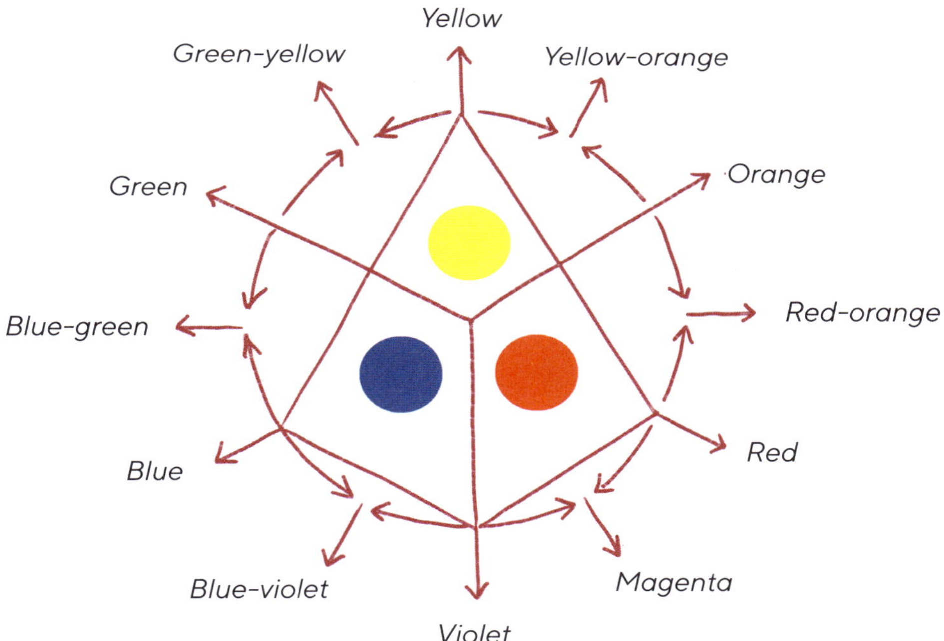

Making a Newton's Disk

Isaac Newton was the first physicist to explain the scientific rules of color. He proved that sunlight is the sum of all the colors in the spectrum. Newton pointed a beam of white light at a prism, which split white light split into seven colors – the colors of the rainbow: red, orange, yellow, green, blue, indigo, and violet. When the newly formed color beams went through a second prism, they once again became white light.

Cut out a circle of white card of approximately 5 inches in diameter and divide it into six equal segments. Color in each segment in the following order: red, orange, yellow, green, blue, and violet. Pierce a small hole in the center and push a pencil through the hole. Spin the card on the pencil as quickly as you can.

As you watch, the circle will turn white. This demonstrates that white light contains all the colors of the spectrum in the same way as splitting it with a prism.

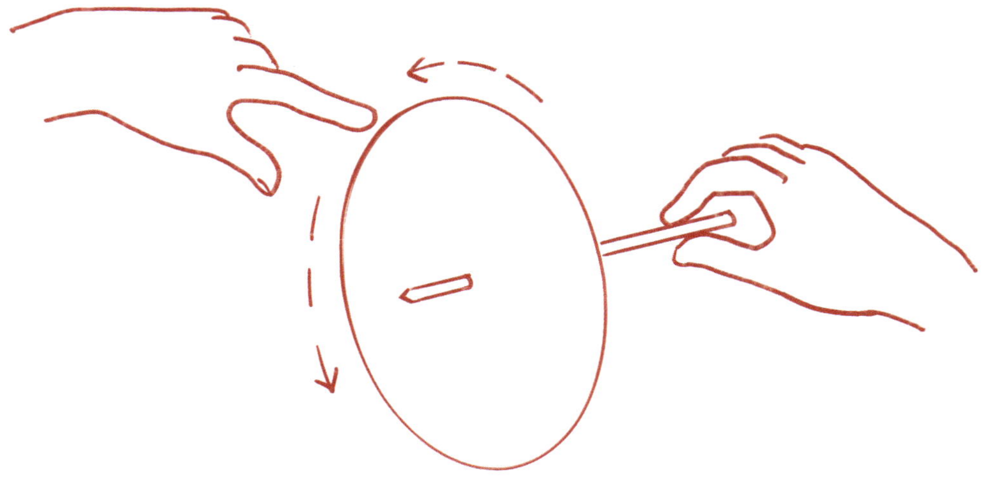

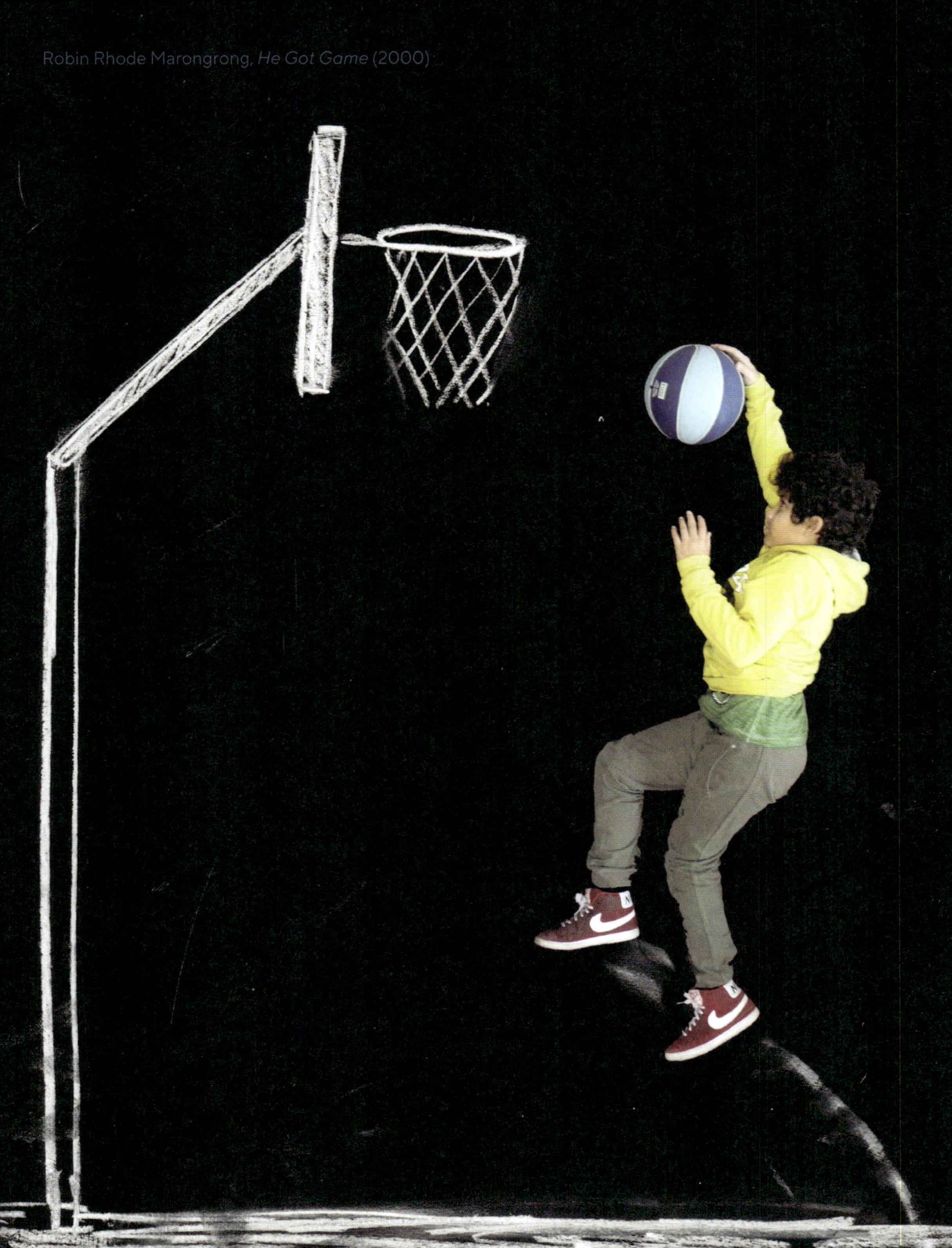

Robin Rhode Marongrong, *He Got Game* (2000)

CHALK

We all know chalk white, the color of the old-fashioned school chalk used for writing or drawing on slate blackboards, replaced long ago with interactive whiteboards. Chalk is a natural limestone, and artists' chalk is actually made from grinding and baking limestone. Even the first cave dwellers used it, and many of our contemporary artists still find it interesting because you can draw anything with a piece of chalk. For example, the artist Robin Rhode combines realistic photos with his chalk drawings, creating new and unexpected images.

Throw the Dice
You can do this, too. Take a photo of your hand while throwing the dice drawn in the picture. Alternatively, you could take a photo of your hand, then draw in something in chalk.

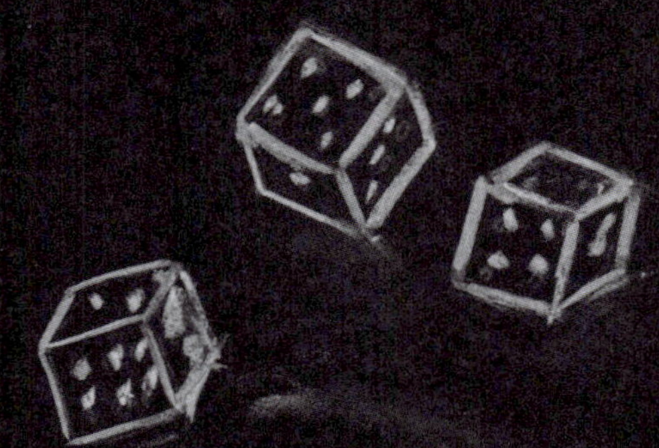

Using Chalk

Use these black backgrounds to experiment with white chalk or white pencil. Try creating static objects and objects, like the dice, that convey movement. Work out ways of showing texture and see whether you prefer drawing rounded or geometric shapes.

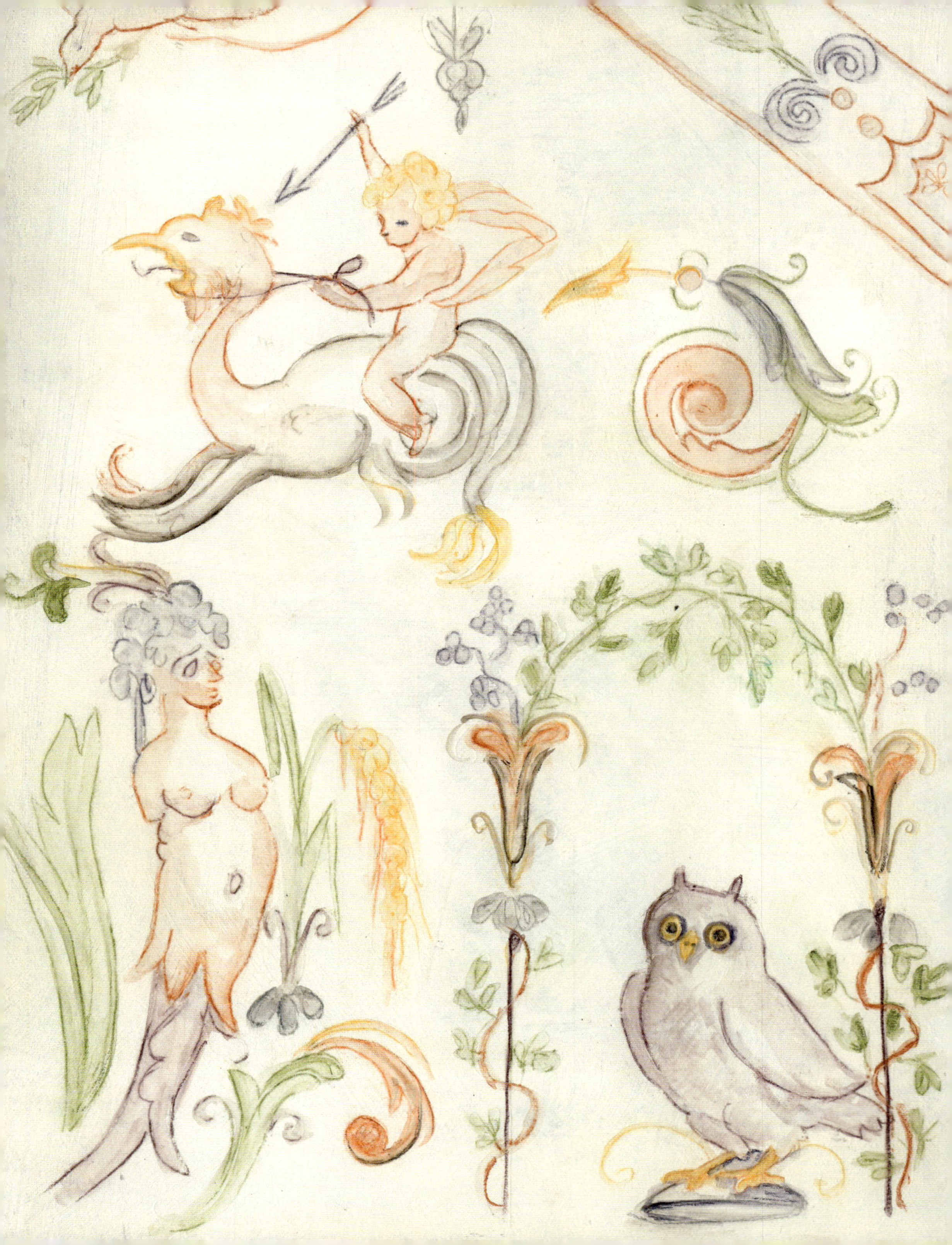

SAINT JOHN'S WHITE

In the past, the most famous white was what the Italian Renaissance artist Cennino Cennini called *Bianco di San Giovanni* (St John's white), in honor of the patron saint of Florence, Saint John the Baptist. Made from slaked lime, it was perfect for painting frescoes but also for painting on wood. We often find it mixed with other colors to obtain paler or luminous effects on clothing, faces, and landscapes.

We seldom see this white on its own, except in the vaults at the Uffizi Gallery, where it provides a background for eccentric decorations: grotesques – ornamental patterns winding around plants, human forms, animals, masks, and architectural features.

Observing and Copying
Observing is the fundamental of drawing and painting. Look at the detail in these paintings and copy some of them as accurately as you can.

Ridolfo del Ghirlandaio, *Grotesques* (1579–1581), Uffizi Gallery, Florence

Create Your Own Grotesques

Renaissance artists had fun using grotesques to invent dream landscapes, monsters, and strange forms. Try mixing flowers, leaves, animals, and imaginary characters to create a world where everything is possible. Paint some on a white background, then paint in white on a darker background and discover different effects.

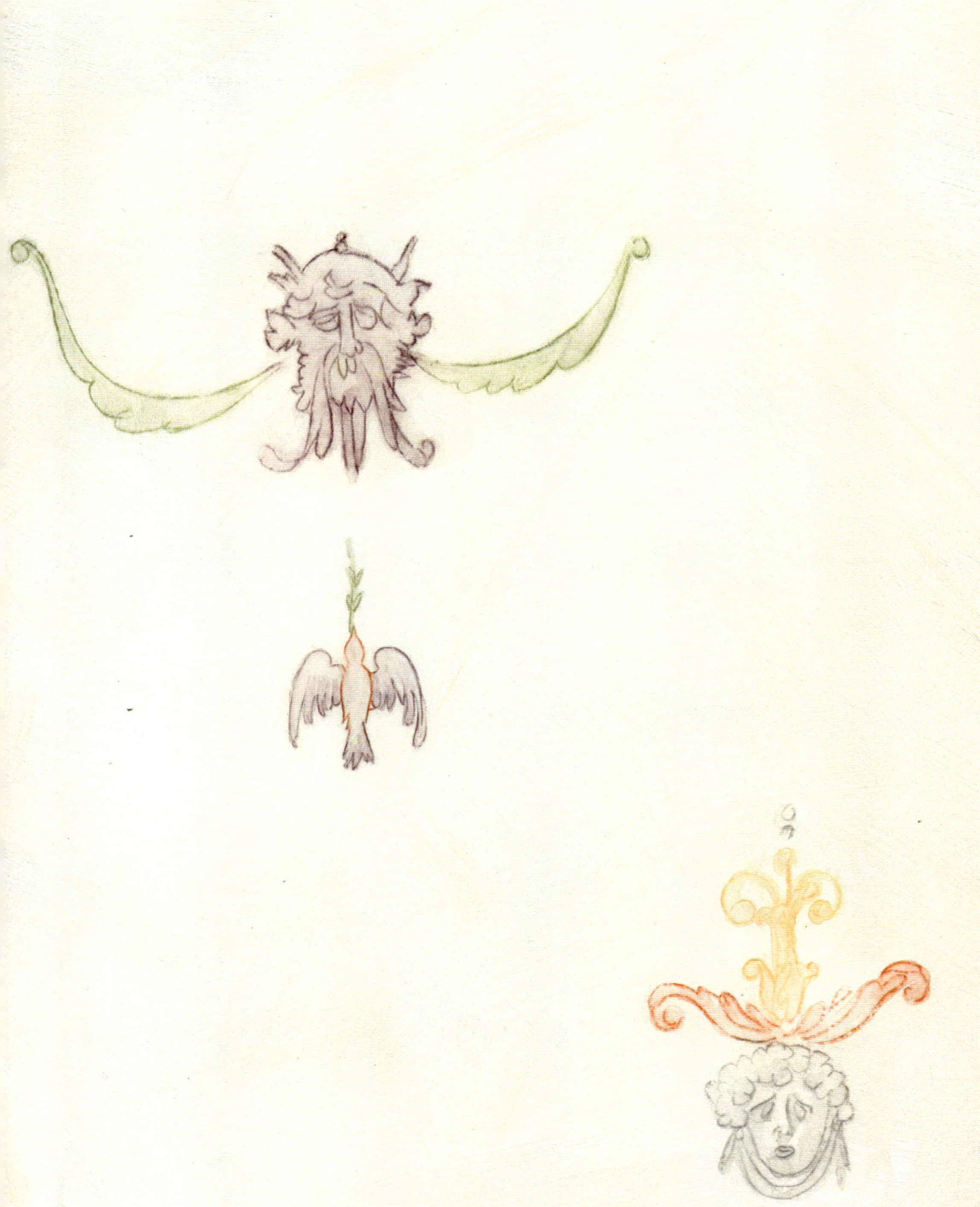

WHITE ON WHITE

Another white that was also widely used in the past was white lead. Being extracted from lead, however, it was toxic, so in the late 18th century, people tried to replace it with zinc white. This was both more expensive and less effective and both zinc and lead white continued to be used until about a century ago, when titanium white appeared and white lead fell into disuse once and for all.

Meanwhile, artists had already drifted away from imitating nature and gone in search of perceptions and pure forms, as in the case of *White on White* by the Russian painter Kazimir Malevich, in which white is an infinite world where you can navigate and lose yourself.

Kazimir Severinovich Malevich, *White on White* (1918), Museum of Modern Art, New York

 ## *Shades of White*

Create a work of art by discovering as many shades of white as you can distinguish. Look for fabrics, paper, card, and plastic in many various whites. Cut them up into geometrical forms and make a composition around the red dot.

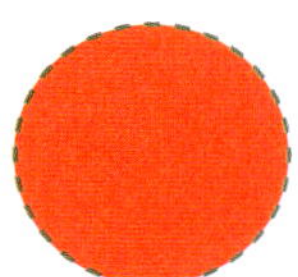

CUTTING THROUGH TO THE TRUTH

In the 20th century, white becomes absolute: it has value *per se* and contains everything.

For Lucio Fontana, white represented the perfect form of our thoughts and notions before being ripped open. His holes and cuts on the canvas suggest that the space for the painting is now obsolete and that a new world awaits us behind the canvas. He writes, "... so I pierce this canvas and create an infinite dimension, because infinity passes through it, light passes through it, and there's no need to paint."

Paper Cuts
Imitating Fontana's work, create an image using just one or two bold slashes through the paper. Does that represent infinity to you? How else would you show infinity?

Lucio Fontana, *Spatial Concept. Waiting* (1965), Museo Novecento, Florence

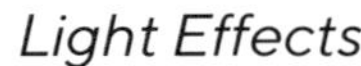

Light Effects

This uses numerous small holes in the paper or canvas. By placing it in front of a light source, it creates an infinite variety of patterns.

Take a white sheet of paper, put it down on a soft surface and makes holes in it with a sharp pencil or ball-point pen, creating the shape you want. Then place it next to a source of light and observe the light and shade effects on both sides of the paper surface. What do they suggest to you?

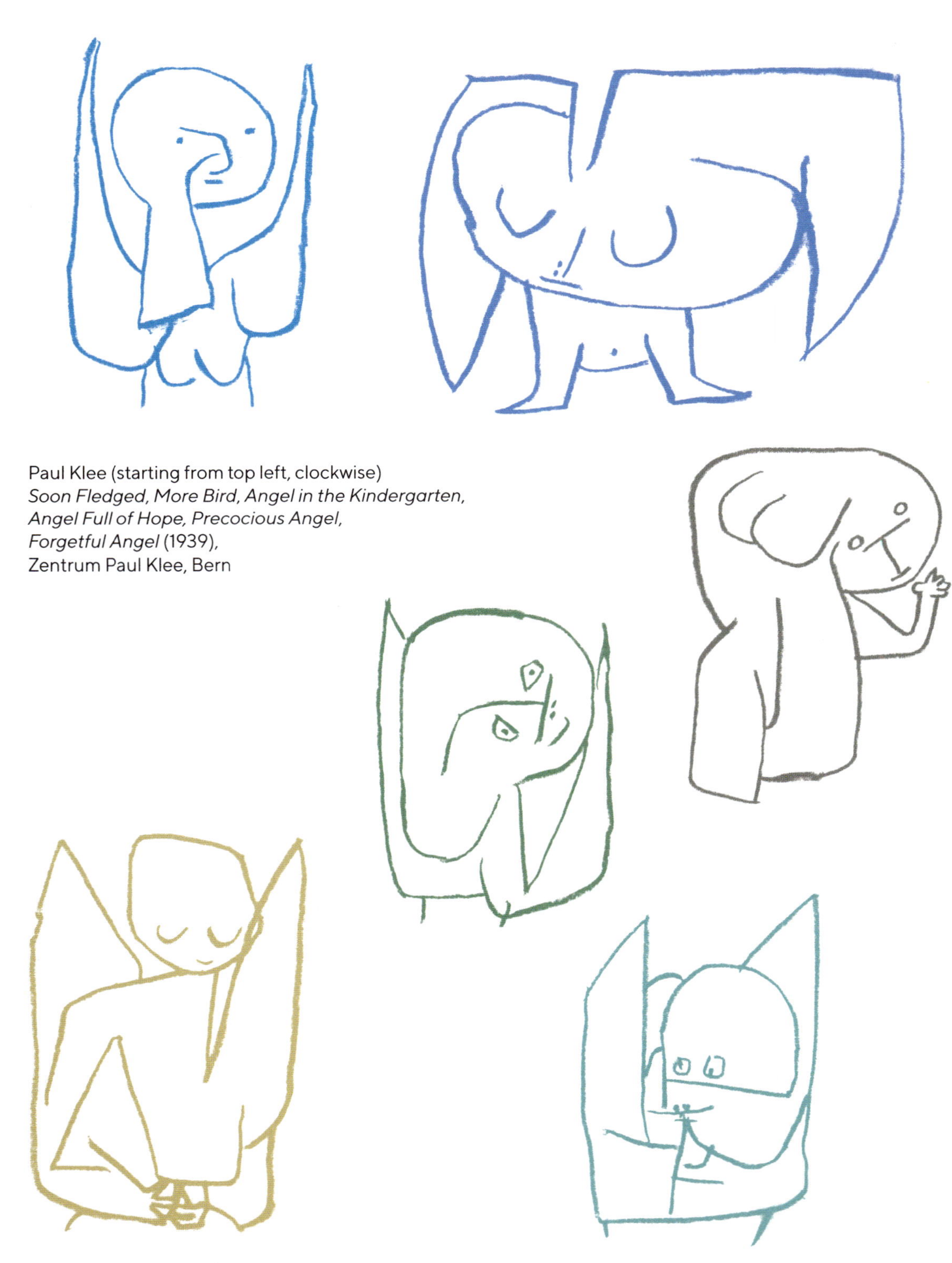

Paul Klee (starting from top left, clockwise)
Soon Fledged, More Bird, Angel in the Kindergarten,
Angel Full of Hope, Precocious Angel,
Forgetful Angel (1939),
Zentrum Paul Klee, Bern

ANGELS

In painting, white has always symbolized something beyond the human world, something divine. In the Christian tradition, white is the Everlasting God, the dove of the Holy Ghost, the clothes of Christ resurrected and the Virgin Mary's assumption into the sky. It is also the color of the lily the Archangel Gabriel proffers to Mary. In these cases, white represents light, purity and innocence.

Archangels, mysterious winged messengers, are also white. Many ancient and modern artists have painted them. Paul Klee, in particular, drew many guardian angels.

Reveal Your Personal Angel
Even if you've never seen an angel, try drawing one – invisible to all except you – as it accompanies you during the day, at school, at home, in the street, and wherever you go.

MYTHICAL CREATURES

The novel *Moby Dick* is about a large, mysterious white whale. In this case, the author chose to use white to represent evil. As a matter of fact, it's the whale that kills Captain Ahab. In most cases, however, white is a symbol of purity and nobility: heroes, kings, and warriors of all times have ridden beautiful white horses. Similarly, unicorns and doves can only be white.

Pure White Beasts

Draw a pure white mythical creature from your own imagination. Many mythical animals combine features of several different, unrelated species so you may want to look for inspiration there.

The Lady and the Unicorn (late 15th century),
Musée national du Moyen Âge de l'Hôtel de Cluny, Paris

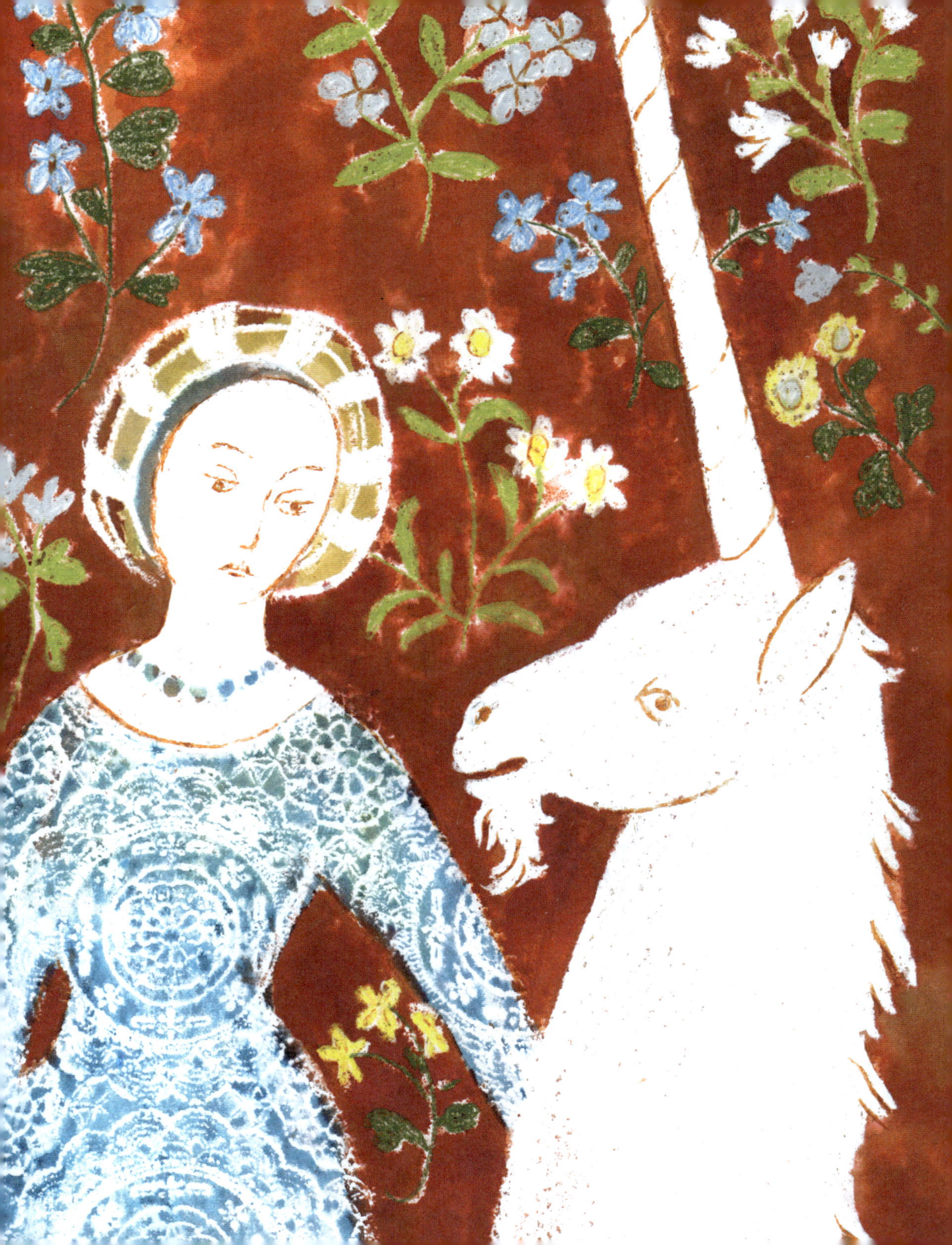

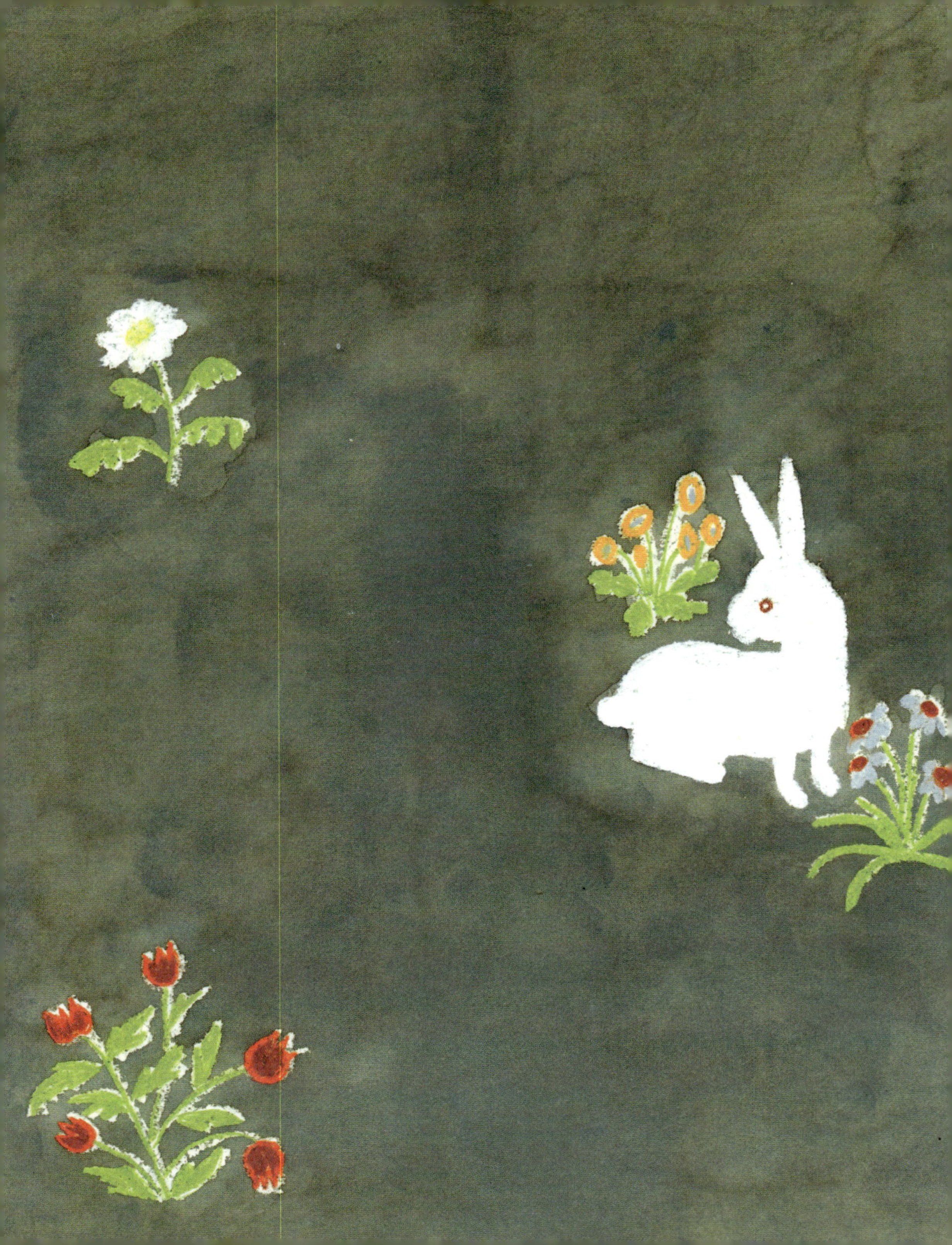

Creating a Tapestry

In the series of medieval tapestries devoted to the Lady and the Unicorn, many white animals feature in the flowery meadow: rabbits, ermines, dogs, foxes, lambs, and so on. Look up the pictures of these tapestries on the internet, observe them carefully then, using a white crayon, try drawing on the meadow the animals you find.

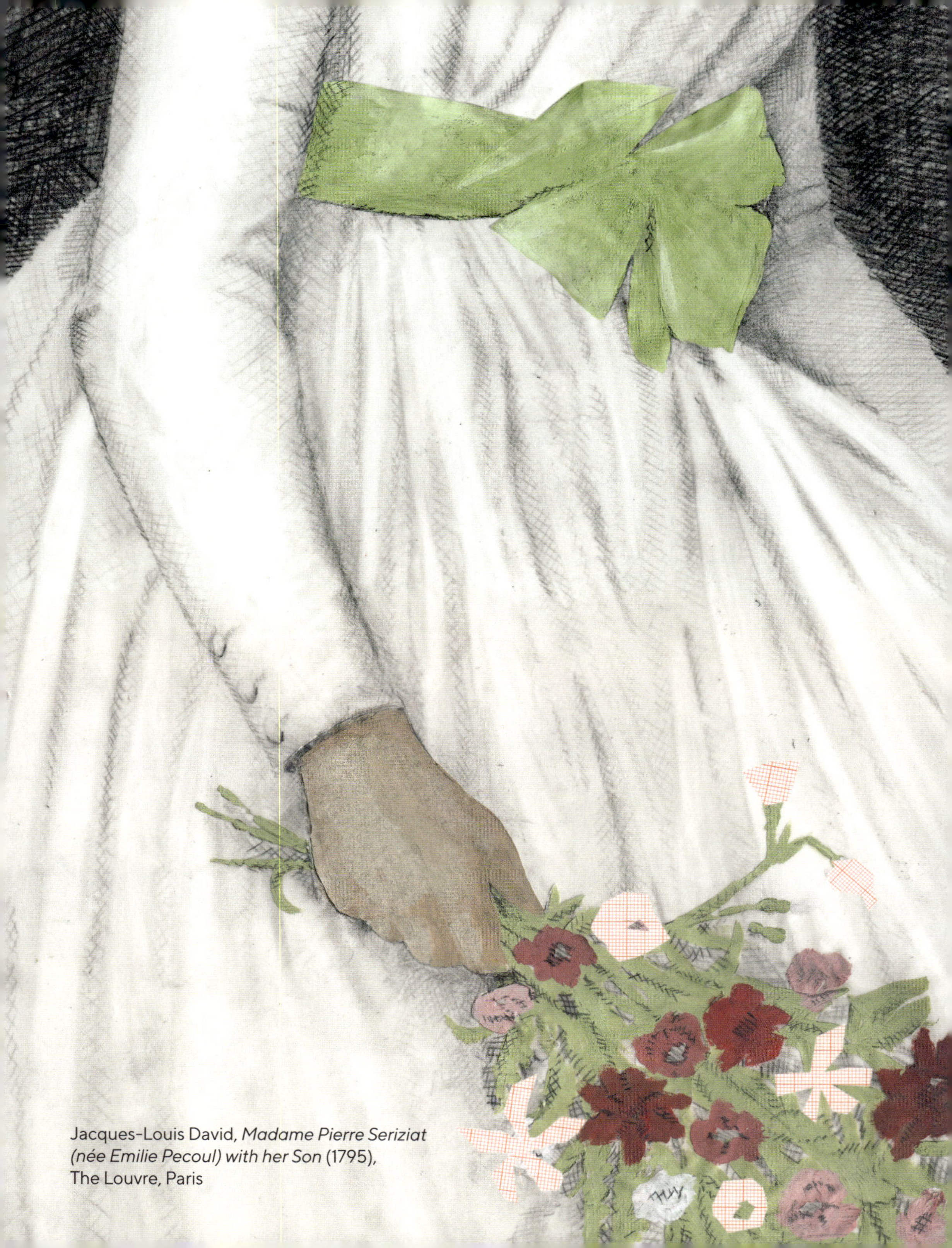

Jacques-Louis David, *Madame Pierre Seriziat (née Emilie Pecoul) with her Son* (1795), The Louvre, Paris

WHITE FABRICS

In every age, wealthy and aristocratic ladies have worn fine white dresses: dresses in which white competes with white, plays with reflections of light, transparency, soft folds and pale-colored lace, in a mixture of fabrics such as silk, velvet, and fur.

Textured Fabrics
Look at how beautifully David has painted the folds of the fabric in the dress. Try to reproduce a similar image in pencil or paint.

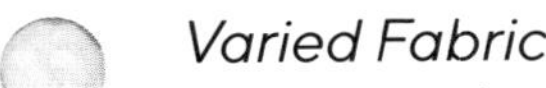

Varied Fabrics

Then try to draw or paint various different fabrics: silk, shiny satin, rich velvet, translucent organza.

Bridal Gowns

Even nowadays, the typical bridal outfit in the West is white. Try to pay attention to the windows of bridal stores in your city. You will notice the large number of possible options: short dresses, long dresses, plain, lavish, matt, and sparkling. In order to create them, the designers have drawn inspiration from clothes from various epochs and countries.

Do the same: find inspiration in a century and a style and then draw in every detail of a dress nobody has yet imagined. Incorporate the most successful of your textural experiments.

PURE AND CLEAN

White is known for another characteristic: it is the symbol of cleanliness.

Our bedsheets, towels and underwear are frequently white, and when a T-shirt is very white we all know that it's clean. It was the same in the past; even though people did not take baths all that often, they were considered clean if they wore a white shirt under their clothes.

Over time, shirts became more visible and extravagant, jutting out from people's clothes with all their folds and lace. In Tudor times, collars became so large and decorative that they were called ruffs – and also, jokingly, "lettuces" as they were like salad leaves.

Painting Lacework
Look at the intricate lacework on the lady's collar and try to copy it. Aim to show the crisp, starched nature of the clean, white fabric.

Jacopo Zucchi, *Clelia Farnese* (circa 1570), National Gallery of Ancient Art, Rome

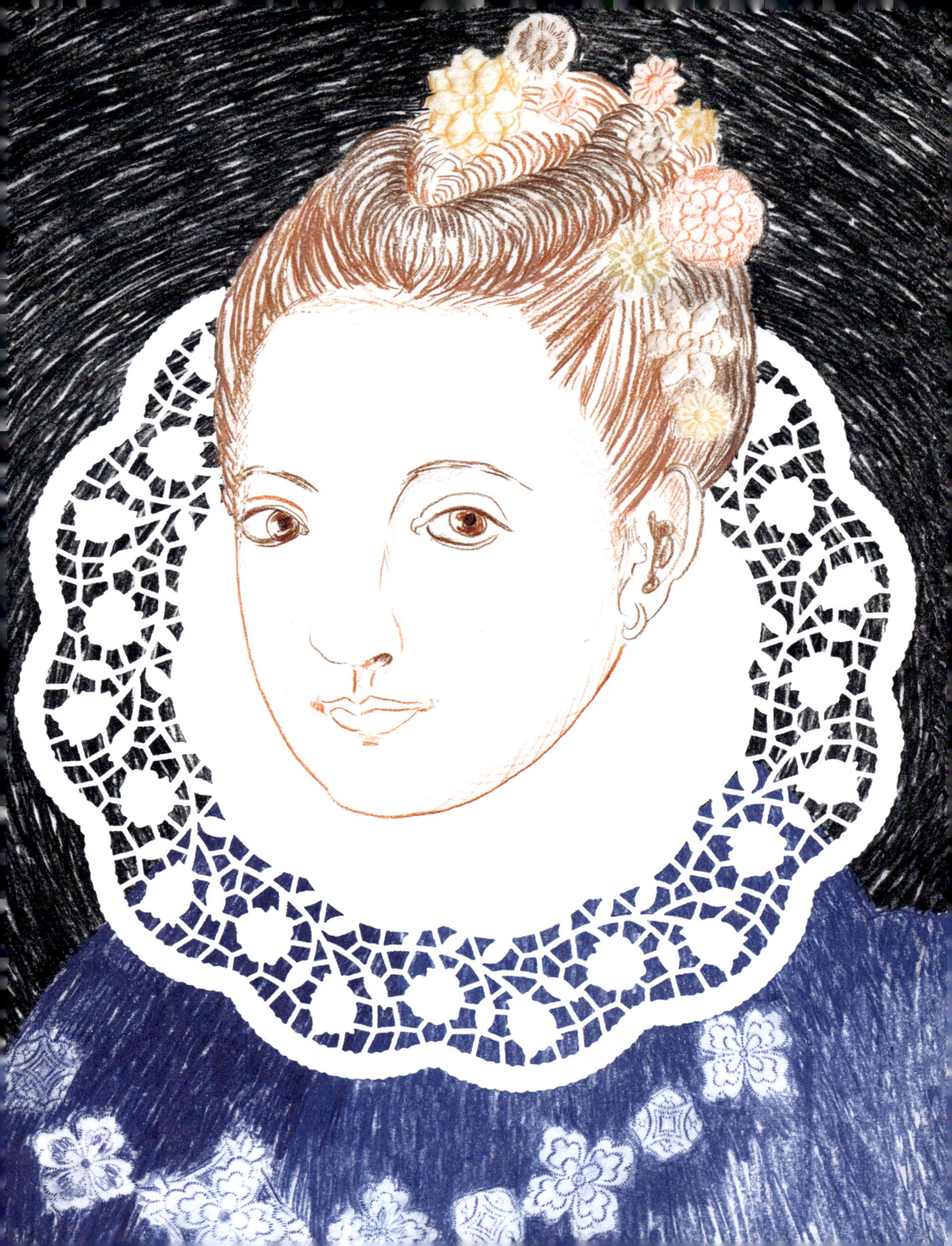

The Elizabethan Ruff

Following the instructions below, try making your own ruff. You can experiment with different thicknesses of paper and more or less narrow folds; you can also discover different ways of cutting the paper in order to create different lace effects.

Divide a sheet of white A4 paper into equal parts, folding it concertina-style. You can use a strip half the width of the paper if you prefer.

Make a hole in the tip and cut into the edge so create a pattern.

Glue several pieces of paper together so you have enough to go comfortably around your neck.

Thread a ribbon through the hole and put on your ruff.

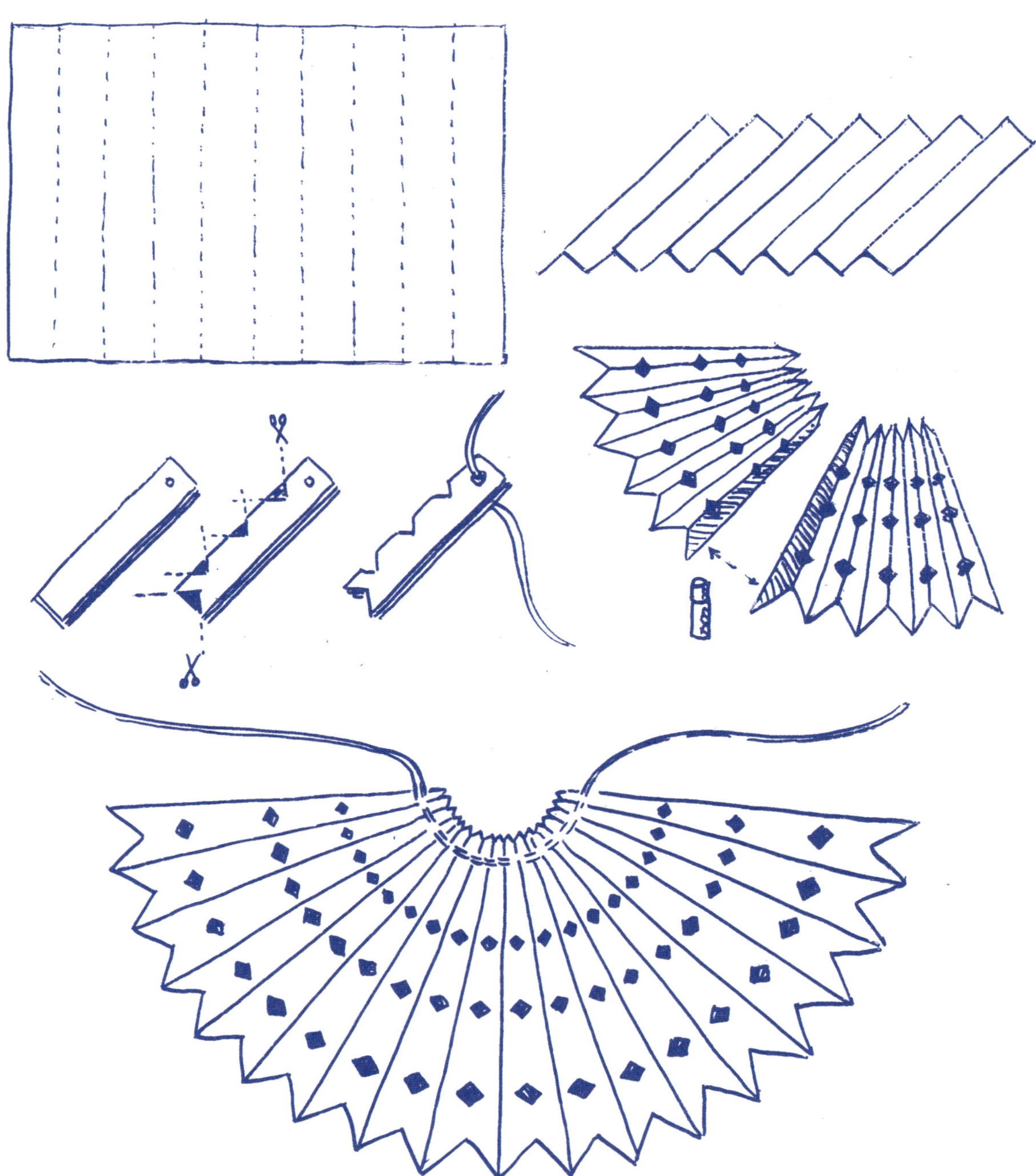

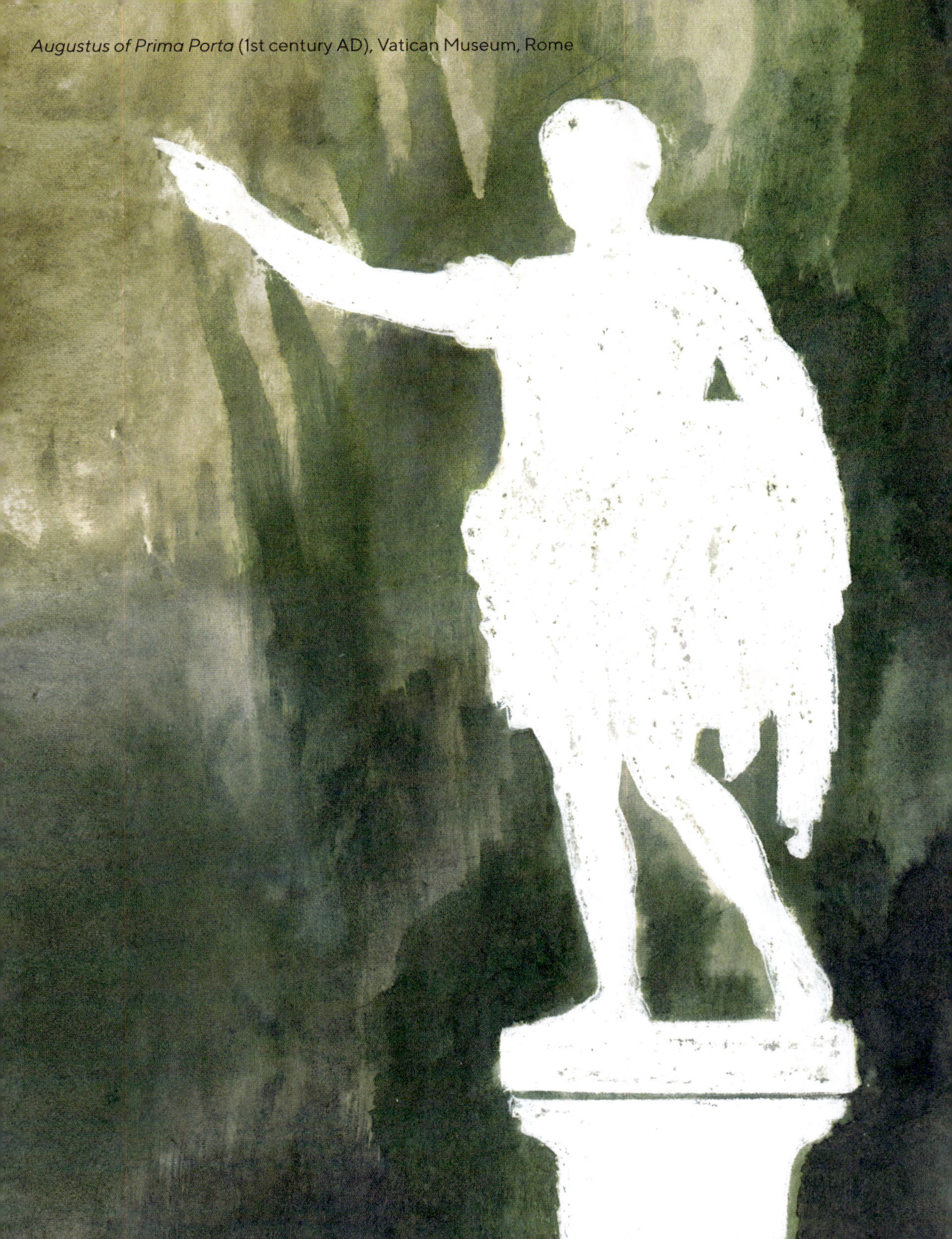

Augustus of Prima Porta (1st century AD), Vatican Museum, Rome

BRINGING STATUES TO LIFE

For centuries, people believed that ancient statues had been created entirely white because we see that what remains now is marble or other stone. It is only relatively recently that we discovered that these statues would have been painted in bright colors so they would look realistic enough to seem alive.

One of these is the statue of Emperor Augustus, called "Prima Porta" after the place where it was discovered.

The emperor is standing up, wearing a richly ornate armour-plate, holding up his arm to request silence before inciting his army to battle.

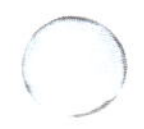

Introducing Color
Take your pencils and try coloring the statue the way it must have been in the past, with red lips, brown hair, and a red and blue armour-plate.

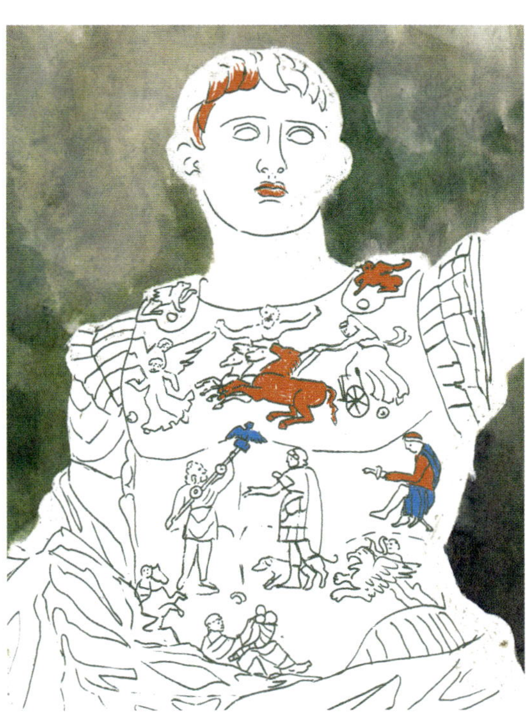

THE STATUE OF NEPTUNE

By imitation, the most famous statues in the Renaissance were stark white, sculpted from white Carrara marble, just like Michelangelo's celebrated *David*, as well as the statues standing next to him in Piazza della Signoria, in Florence.

Among them stands Bartolomeo Ammannati's *Neptune*. Florentines did not like him when they first saw him. He was a true white colossus, too white; so much so that he was immediately rechristened "the white giant". Surrounded by sea creatures, Neptune is in a chariot drawn by sea-horses.

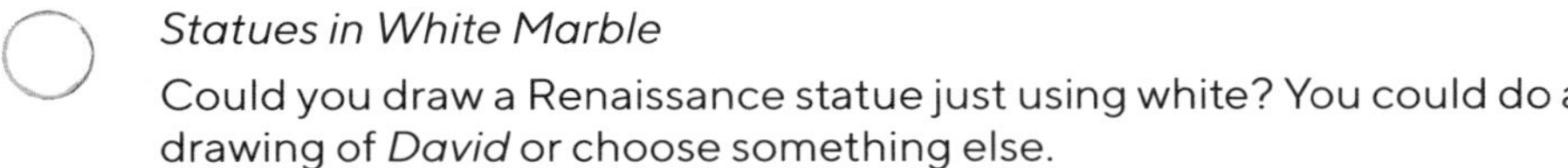

Statues in White Marble
Could you draw a Renaissance statue just using white? You could do a drawing of *David* or choose something else.

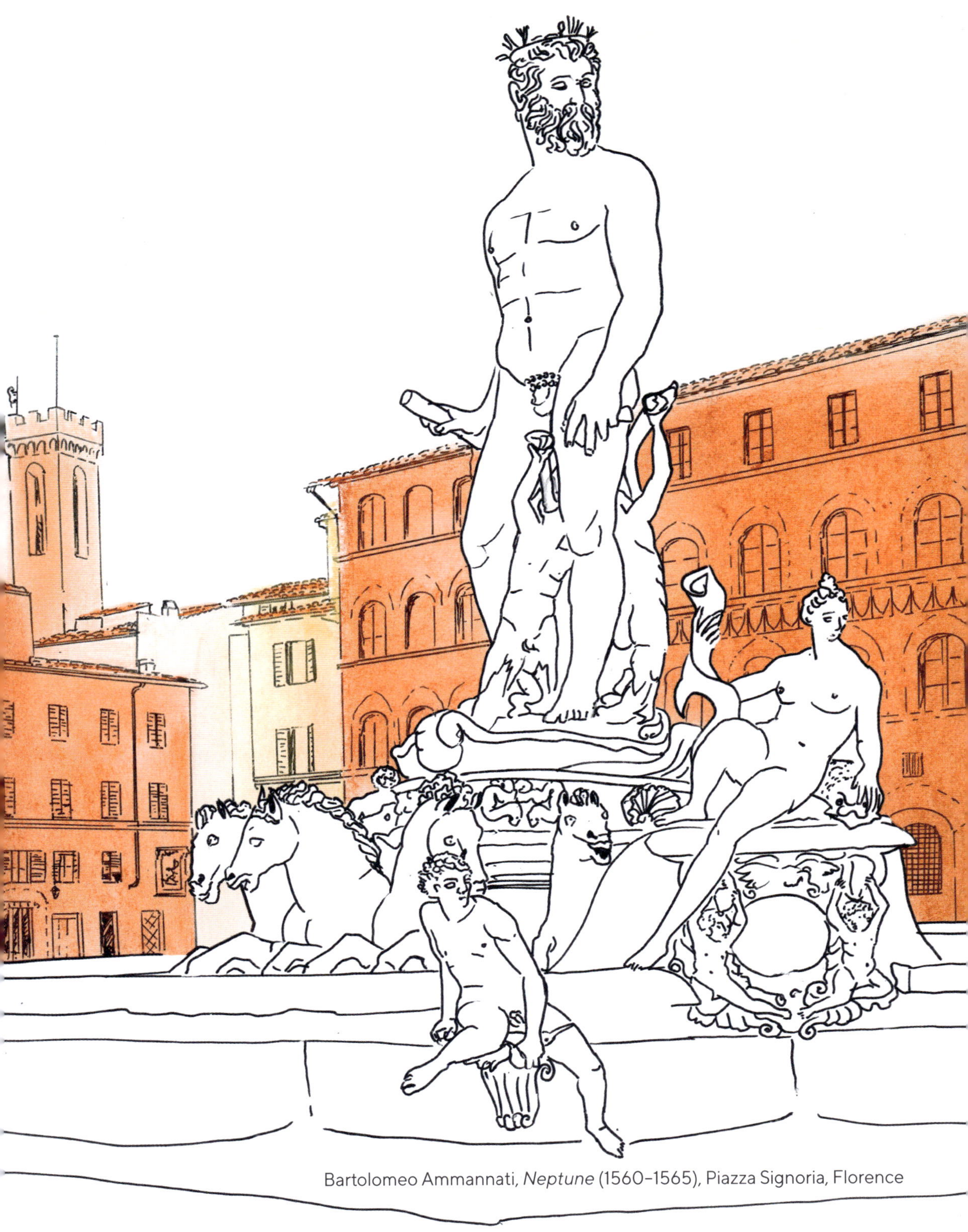

Bartolomeo Ammannati, *Neptune* (1560–1565), Piazza Signoria, Florence

Decorative Elements for a Fountain

Here are some ideas for the elements of a decorative found in the Renaissance style. Cut out the decorations, shells and fish and design a fountain in a similar style, or else draw your own below.

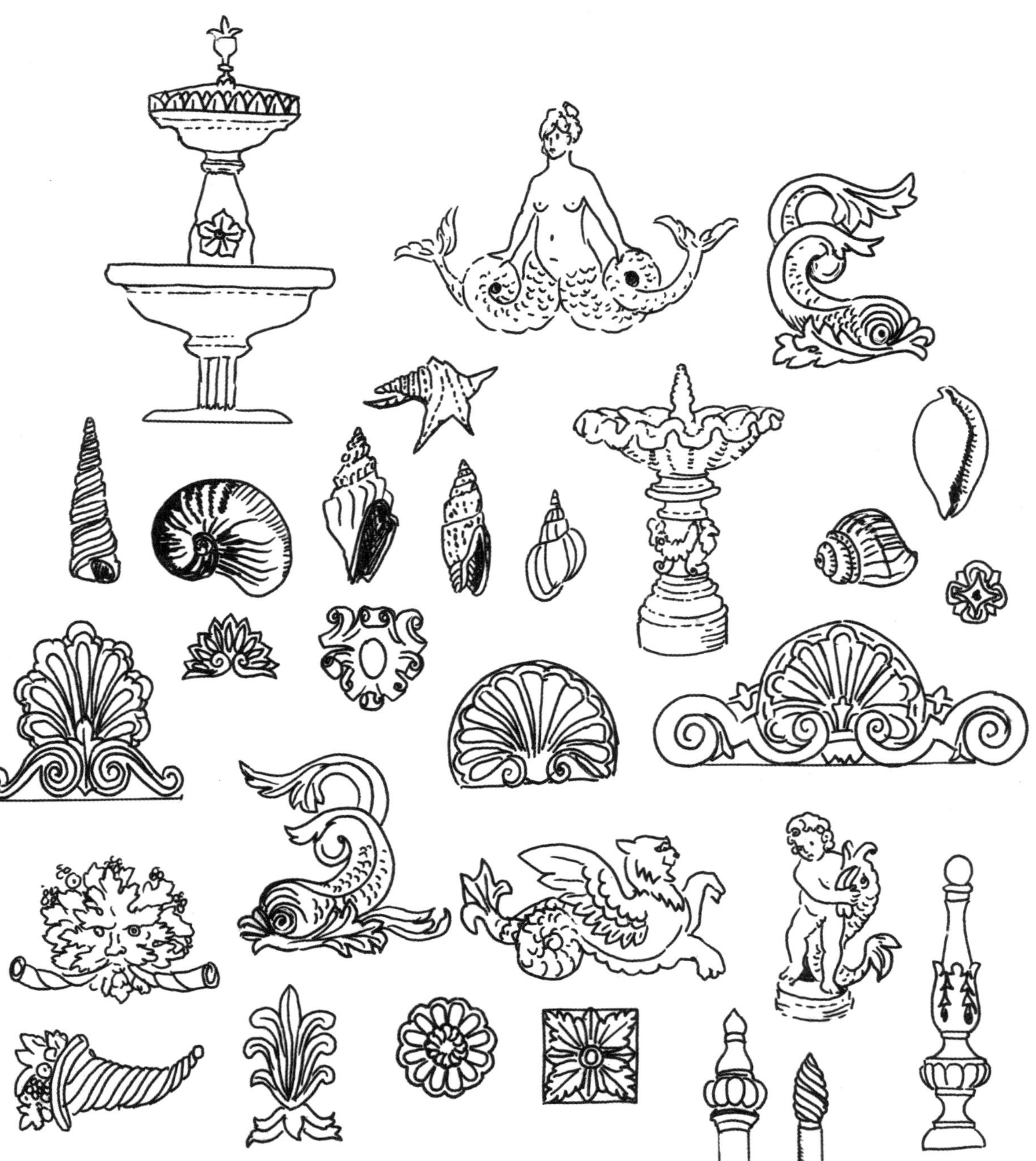

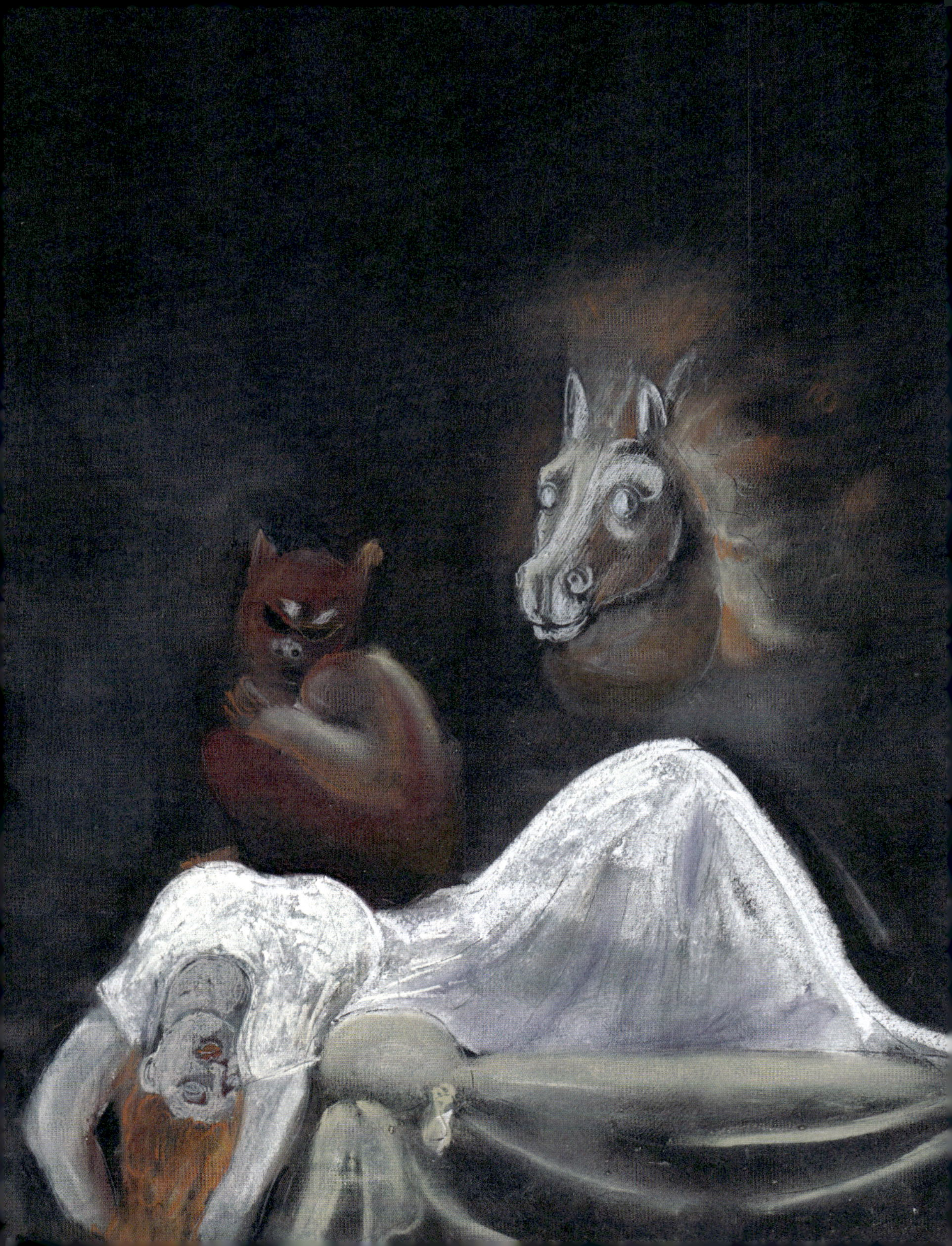

CREATURES OF THE NIGHT

The creatures that populate our nights (not necessarily traditional ghosts) are also often white. The characters that inhabit our dreams are impalpable, intangible, and practically transparent because they are not part of the real world and vanish as soon as we wake up. Just like the creatures painted by the Romantic painter Johann Heinrich Füssli, mysterious, transitory, and silent creatures come to life in his world, appearing and disappearing just like dreams do.

Mysterious Creatures
Look at how the artist uses white to create an insubstantial feel to the animals. What are the animals that appear in your dreams? Can you draw them below?

Johann Heinrich Füssli, *The Nightmare* (1871), Detroit Institute of Arts

Bring Your Dream to Life

Try to remember a dream you've had and draw it below, using a white wax crayon. Once you've finished, brush it with a coat of dark watercolor: the drawing will appear as if by magic.

Try drawing your dream on white paper and use a soft edge and blended white to give everything an unreal and ethereal quality.

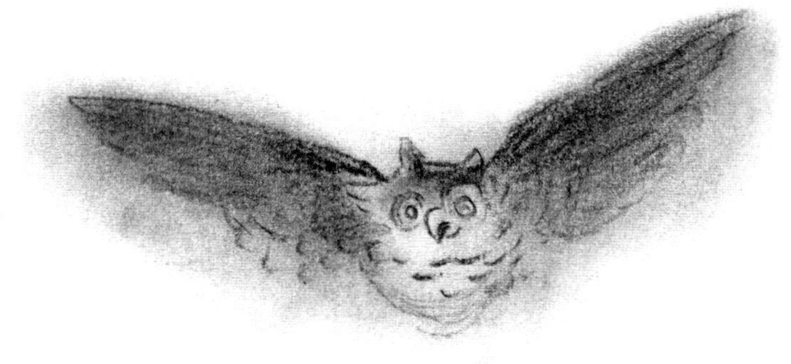

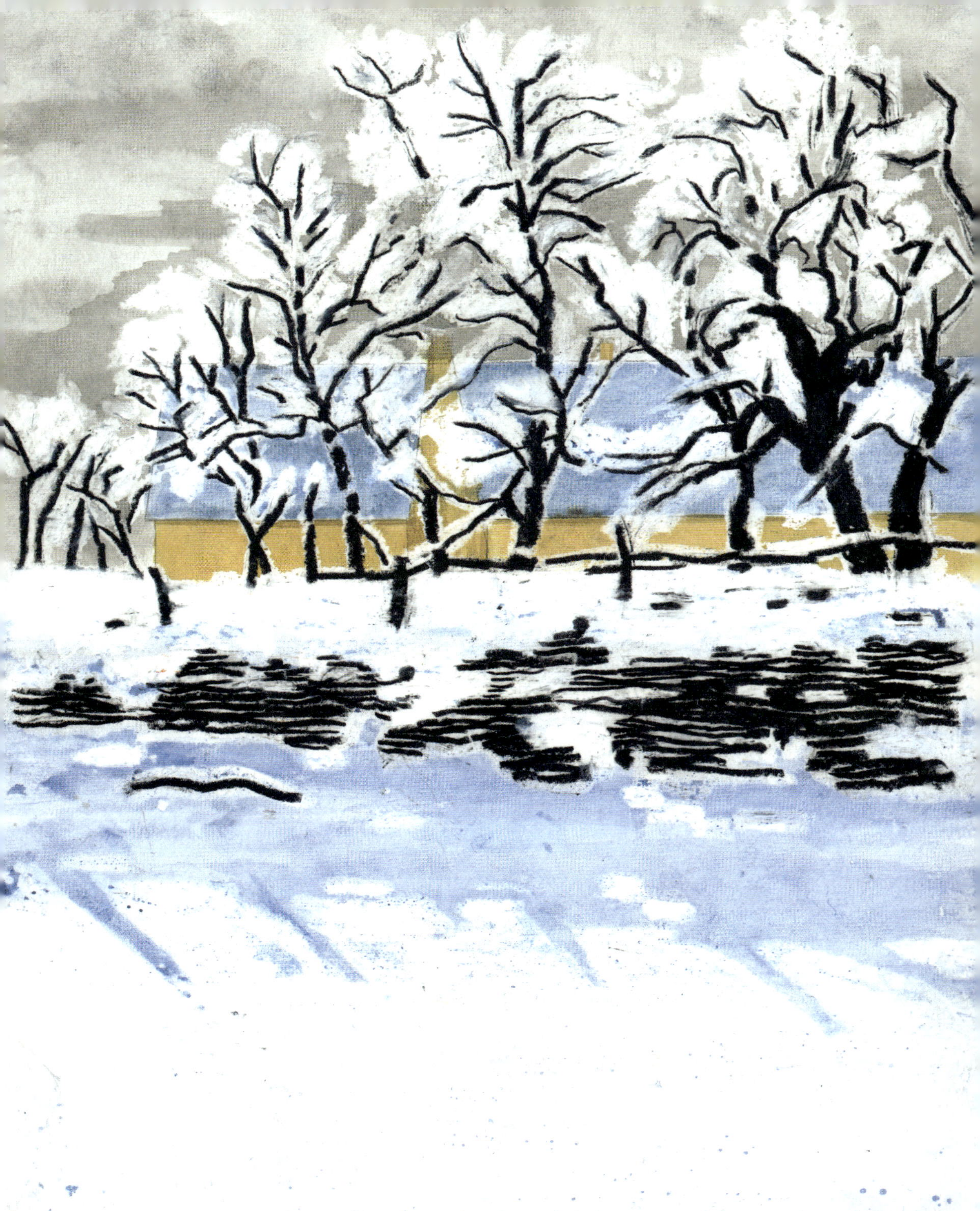

AS WHITE AS SNOW

If we tried to catch a dream creature, we would end up empty-handed, the same way as when we try to hold snow, which is destined to melt after a few seconds. Made up of billions of tiny, transparent ice crystals, snow looks compact, white, soft as a cloak, and produces beautiful light effects. This is why artists of every epoch have loved it and found it challenging to paint; snow is white but it is not only white.

For example, the great Impressionist painter Claude Monet tried to reproduce on the canvas all the color shades reflected, absorbed and taken on by snow.

Snow Scene
Look outside your window. Imagine what the scene would look like covered in snow, and draw or paint this.

Claude Monet, *The Magpie* (1868–1869), Musée d'Orsay, Paris

Unique Snowflakes

Snow crystals have an infinite number of shapes but are always hexagonal. Using this pattern, try inventing new ones.

Try drawing them using different media and using white paper and pencil, and also black paper and chalk or a white colored pencil or pastel.

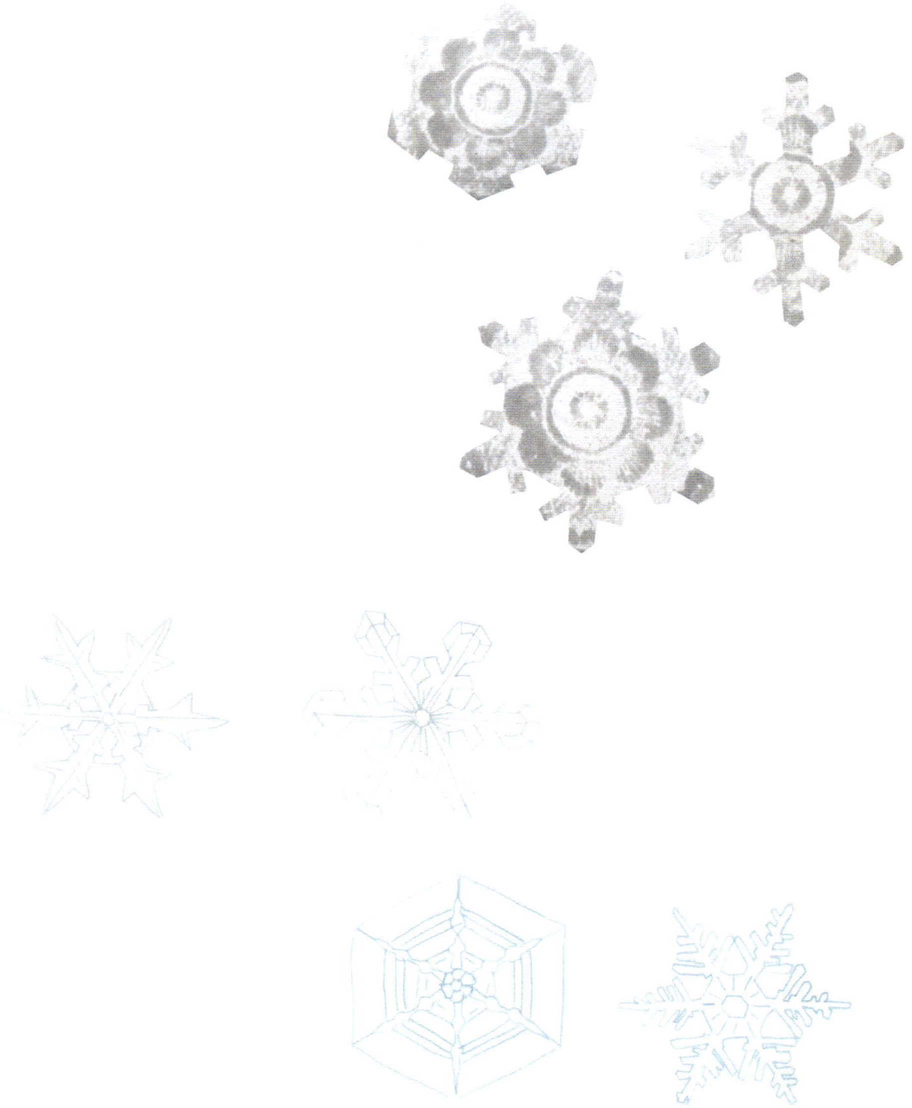

CLOUDY SKIES

Just like snow, clouds are formed of tiny water and ice particles, and can be more or less compact or transparent, lighter or darker.

They are forever changing before our eyes and take on every possible shape: sheep, elephants, ships, lions. It is therefore not surprising that clouds are a true paradise for the imagination, especially that of artists. Among them, John Constable, an English painter who lived from the 18th to the 19th century, stared up at many clouds and painted them numerous times. He would watch them carefully, study how they changed depending on the light, the weather and the air, and try to convey their extraordinary shades on the canvas.

John Constable, *Cloud Studies*, (1821), Royal Academy of Arts, London

Looking at the Sky

Following Constable's example, open the window or go outside and look at the sky. What are the clouds like today? Try drawing them. Decide whether you want to use watercolors, chalk, crayons or pencils: each will give a different effect. If you keep playing this game, you'll become a collector of skies, just like John Constable.

Try to draw the clouds swiftly as they move across the sky, using white to find ways to indicate movement. Look for storm clouds with their dark, towering billows, and contrast them with high wispy clouds in a clear blue sky.

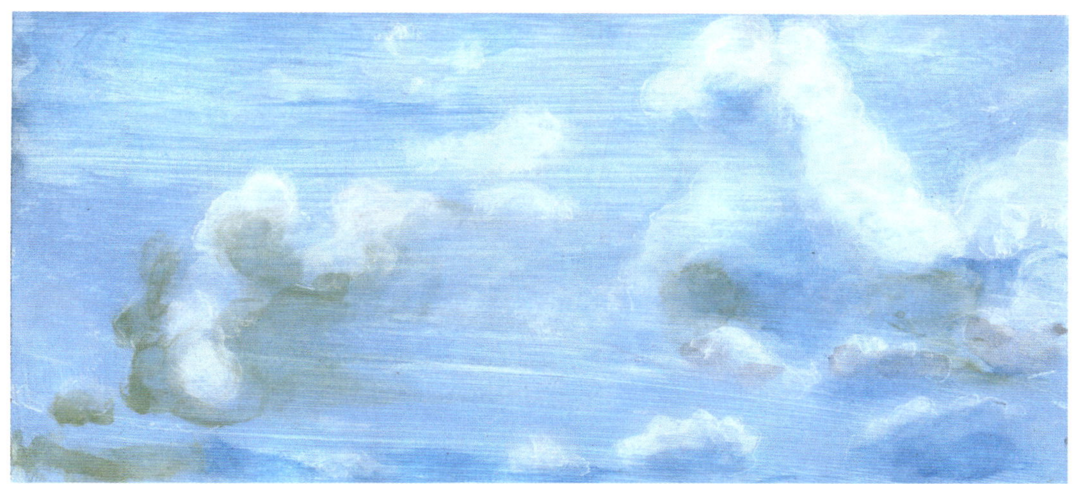

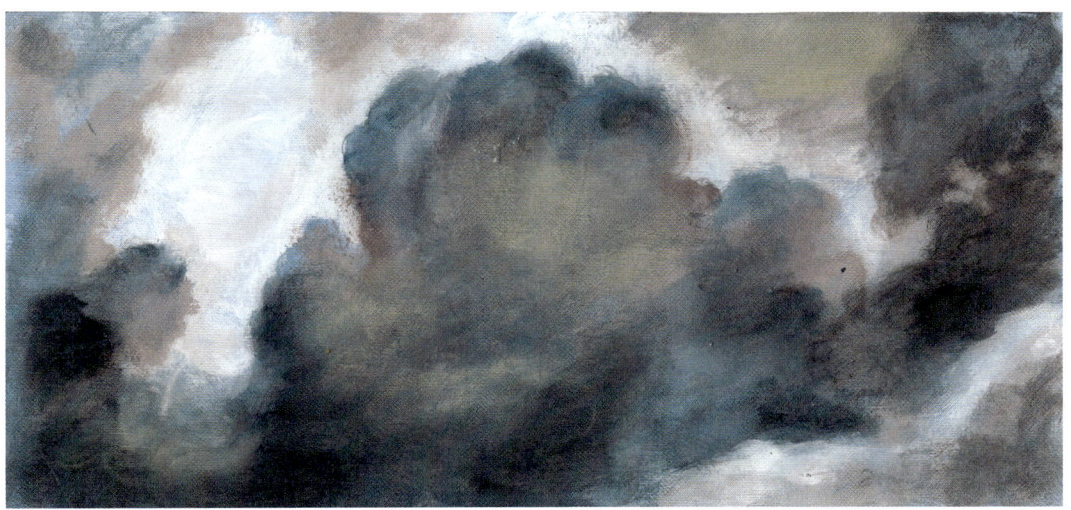

John Constable, *Cloud Studies*, (1822), Victoria and Albert Museum, London

THE BLANK PAGE

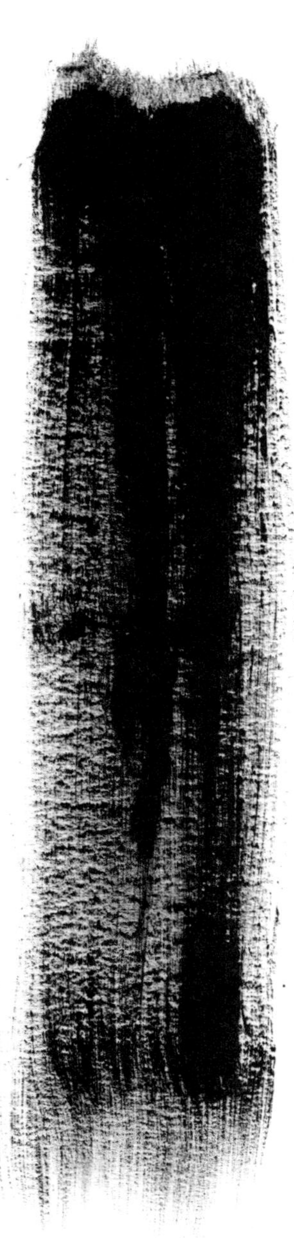

We cannot end without a white, blank page: something that has always frightened artists more than anything else, whether they are poets, painters or novelists. Whenever a pupil would freeze in front of a blank canvas, the Venetian painter Emilio Vedova had an infallible remedy: he would plunge a large brush into a bucket of paint then slap the canvas hard with it. With this gesture, he liberated his pupils from fear, and prompted them to overcome their feeling of intimidation before the uncontaminated, white canvas.

Taking the Plunge
Try doing the same thing: concentrate and look at this blank space. And when you feel that its blank whiteness has made a clean sweep of all your ideas, take the colors and attack: you're the one drawing the end of this book!

PAINTING IN WHITE

Now that this book has ended, try to think of all the white things you know and make a list, from fog to whipped cream, from the Snow Queen to the polar bear, from sugared almonds to eggs and swans. You will realize that white is everywhere and can have many different meanings. Now do this on your own and discover all the white that's around you.

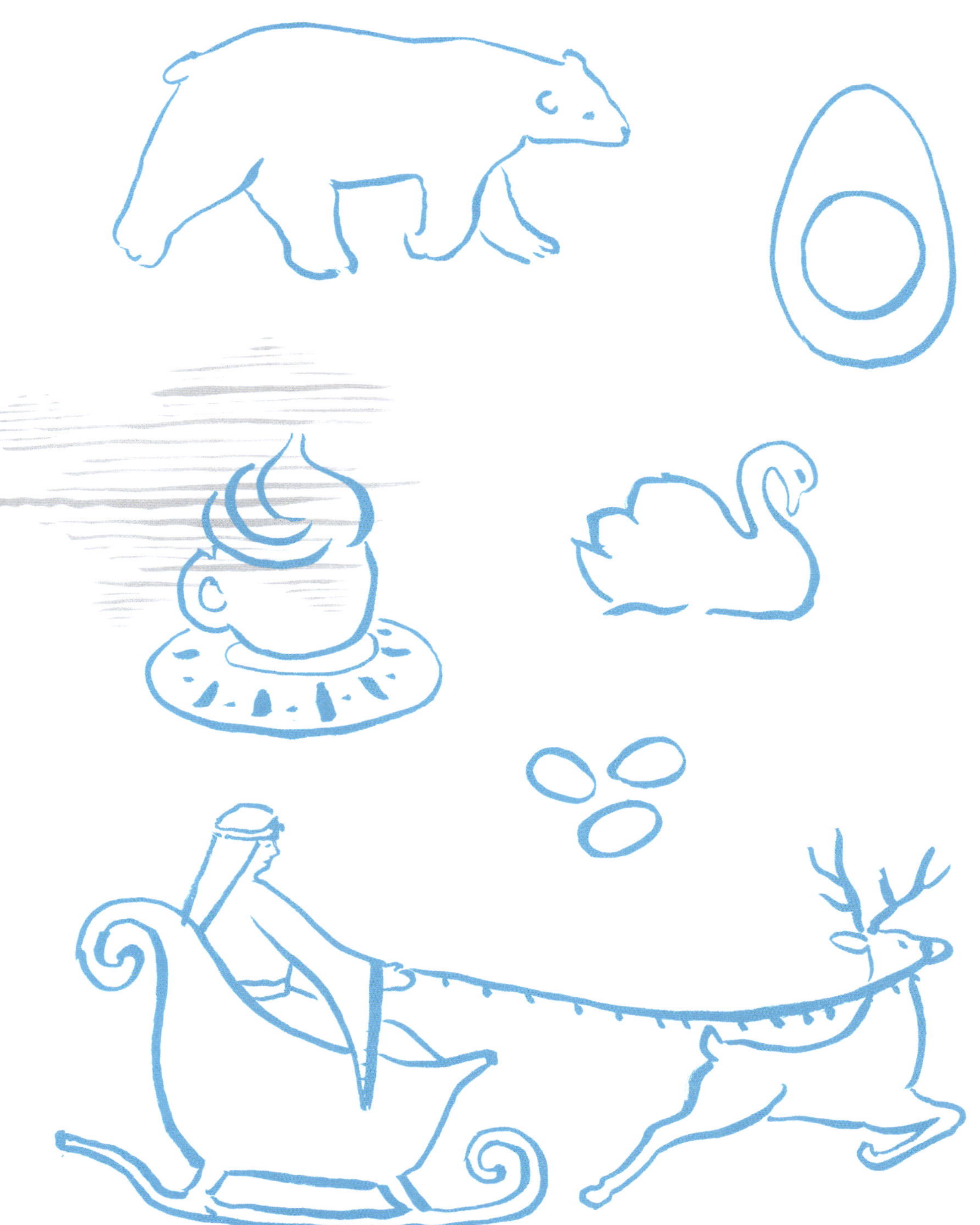

WHERE TO FIND OUT MORE

There is a wealth of information on the internet, in museums and libraries. Use this information as a springboard for your creative exploration of the fascinating world of color.

Bartolomeo Ammannati (1511–1592) Italian architect and sculpture who closely imitated the style of Michelangelo.

Cennino Cennini (c1370–1440) Tuscan painter who published *The craftsman's handbook*, a manual on painting techniques.

John Constable (1776–1837) English landscape painter who revolutionised the genre of landscape painting.

Jacques-Louis David (1748–1825) French painter in the Neoclassical style, widely considered to be pre-eminent in his time.

Lucio Fontana (1899–1968) Argentinian painter, sculptor and theorist.

Johann Heinrich Füssli (1741–1825) Swiss painter also interested in literature and theology.

Ridolfo del Ghirlandaio (1483–1561) Member of a family of artists in Florence, the young Michelangelo was apprenticed to his father.

Johann Wolfgang Goethe (1739–1842) German author and influential literary icon and amateur artist who published *The theory of colors*.

Paul Klee (1879–1940) A Swiss-born German artist whose work explored Expressionism, Cubism and Surrealism.

Kazimir Severinovich Malevich (1879–1935) Avante-guarde artist and theorist.

Claude Monet (1840–1926) French painter and one of the founders of the Impressionist movement, which aimed to capture the artist's immediate perceptions of nature.

Robin Rhode Marongrong (b1976) South African artist based in Berlin.

Henri Matisse (1869–1954) French painter known for his expressive use of color.

Isaac Newton (1642–1727) Highly influential English mathematician and physicist who studied optics, among many other disciplines.

Jacopo Zucchi (c1540–1596) Italian painter and draughtsman who trained under Giorgio Vasari in Florence.

Detroit Institute of Arts, dia.org

The Louvre, Paris, louvre,fr

Musée d'Orsay, Paris, m.musee-orsay.fr/en

Musée National du Moyen Âge de l'Hôtel de Cluny, Paris, musee-moyenage.fr/en/site/the-hotel-de-cluny.html

Museo Novecento, Florence, museonovecento.it/en

Museum of Modern Art, New York, moma.org

National Gallery, London, nationalgallery.org.uk

National Gallery of Ancient Art, Rome, barberinicorsini.org

Palazzo Vecchio, florenceartmuseums.com/palazzo-vecchio

Royal Academy of Arts, London, royalacademy.org.uk

Uffizi Gallery, Florence, uffizi.it

Vatican Museum, Rome, museivaticani.va/content/museivaticani/en.html

Victoria and Albert Museum, London,vam.ac.uk

Yale Center for British Art, New Haven, britishart.yale.edu

Zentrum Paul Klee, Bern, zpk.org

ACKNOWLEDGEMENTS:

The Italian publishers would like to thank MUS.E and Giotto FILA, who partnered with them to make these books possible.

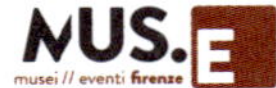 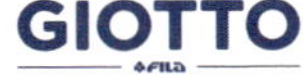

This English language edition Published in 2021 by OH!,
an imprint of Welbeck Non-Fiction Limited,
part of Welbeck Publishing Group
20 Mortimer Street
London W1T 3JW
English Translation by © Welbeck Non-Fiction Limited

First published by © Topipittori Milan in 2016
Original title: *Bianco*
www.topipittori.it

Disclaimer:
All trademarks, quotations, company names, registered names, products, characters, logos and catchphrases used or cited in this book are the property of their respective owners. This book is a publication of OH!, an imprint of Welbeck Publishing Group Limited, and has not been licensed, approved, sponsored, or endorsed by any person or entity.

Bianco by Valentina Zucchi and and Francesca Zoboli
ISBN 978-1-80069-057-8

Text © Valentina Zucchi and Francesca Zoboli
Translator: Katherine Gregor
Editorial: Wendy Hobson
Design: Nikki Ellis
Production: Rachel Burgess

A CIP catalogue record for this book is available from the British Library

Printed and bound in China by Leo Paper Products Ltd.

10 9 8 7 6 5 4 3 2 1